What Parts Do Animals Have?

by Nate George

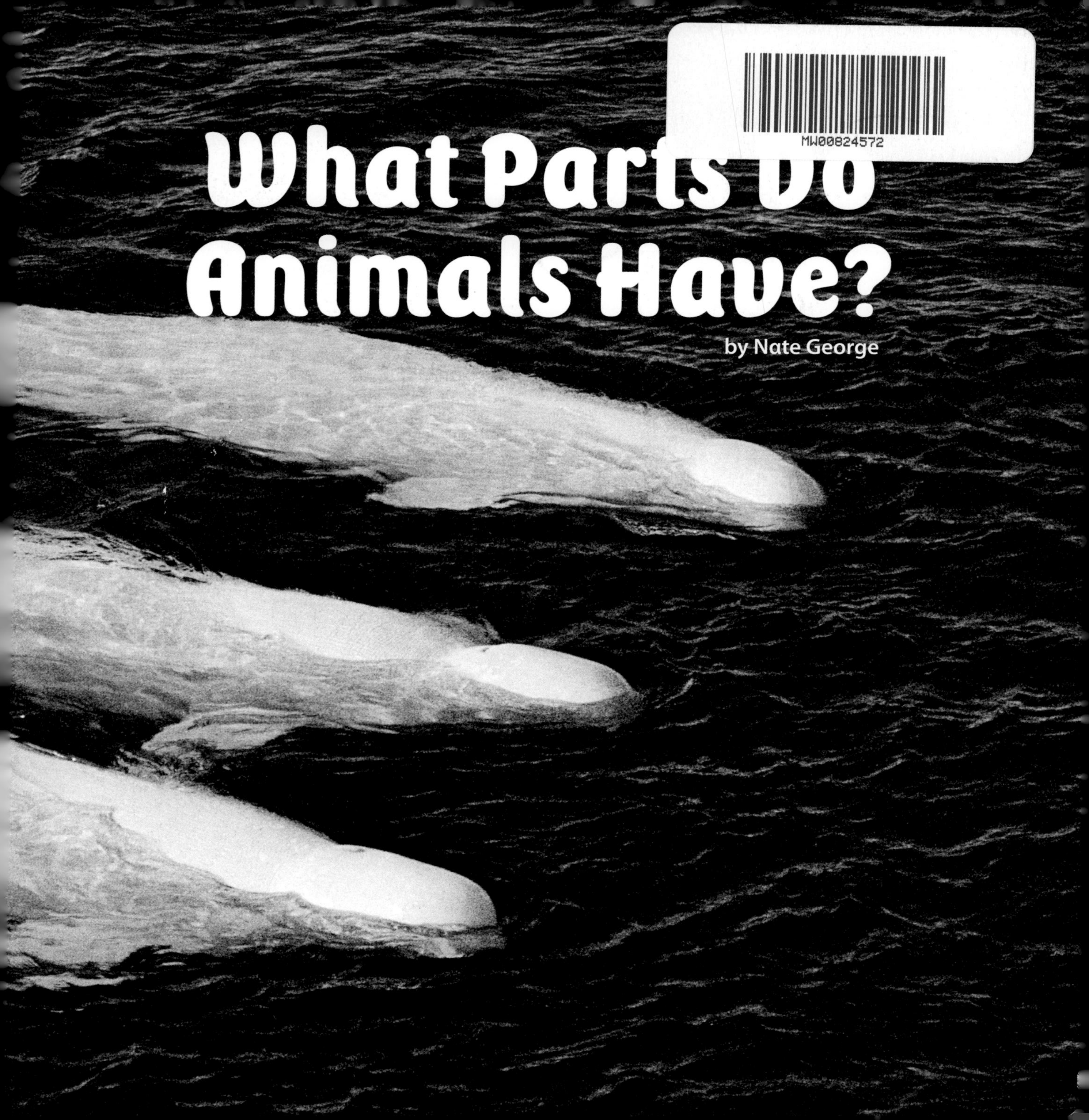

Snowy owl

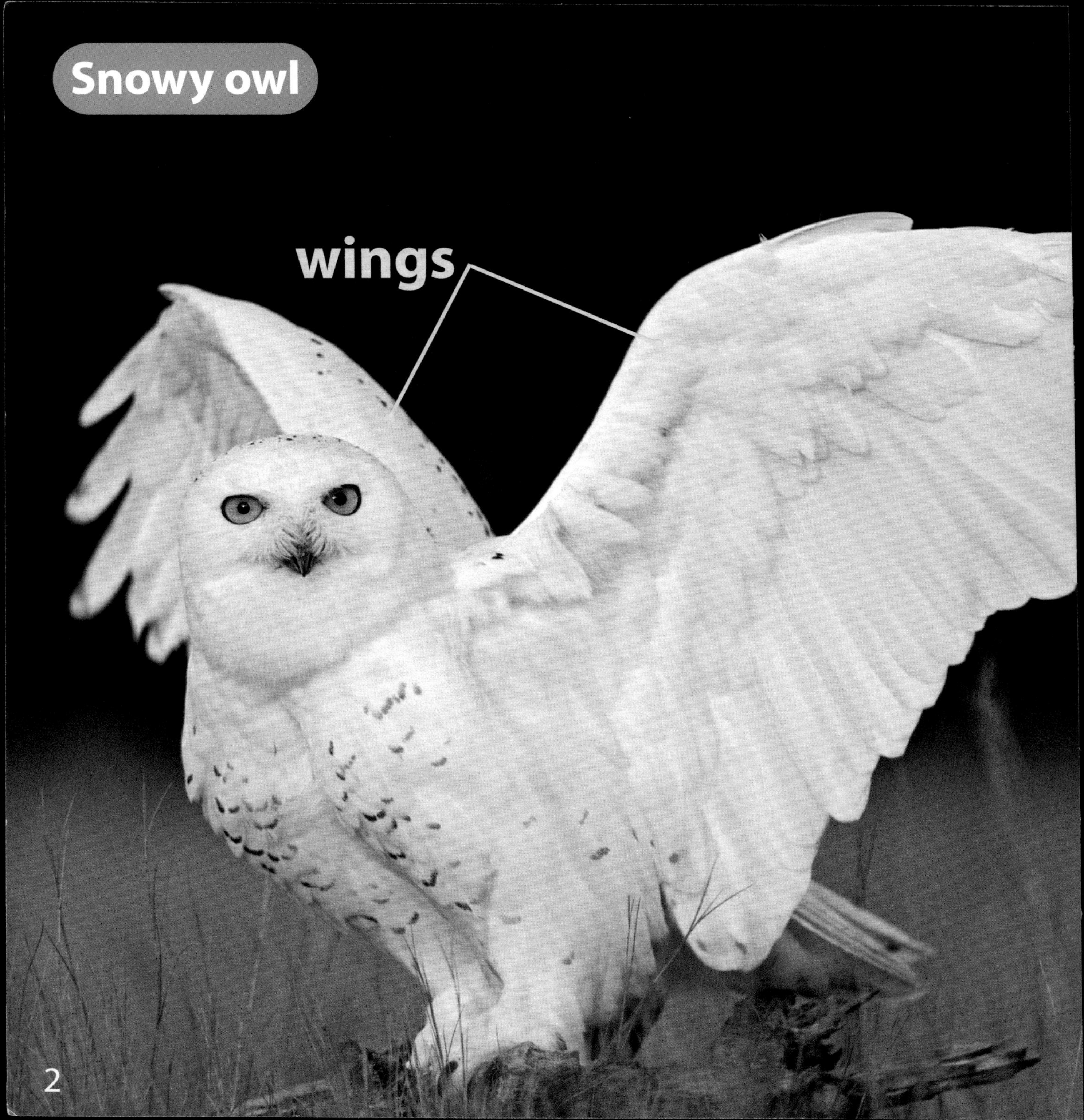

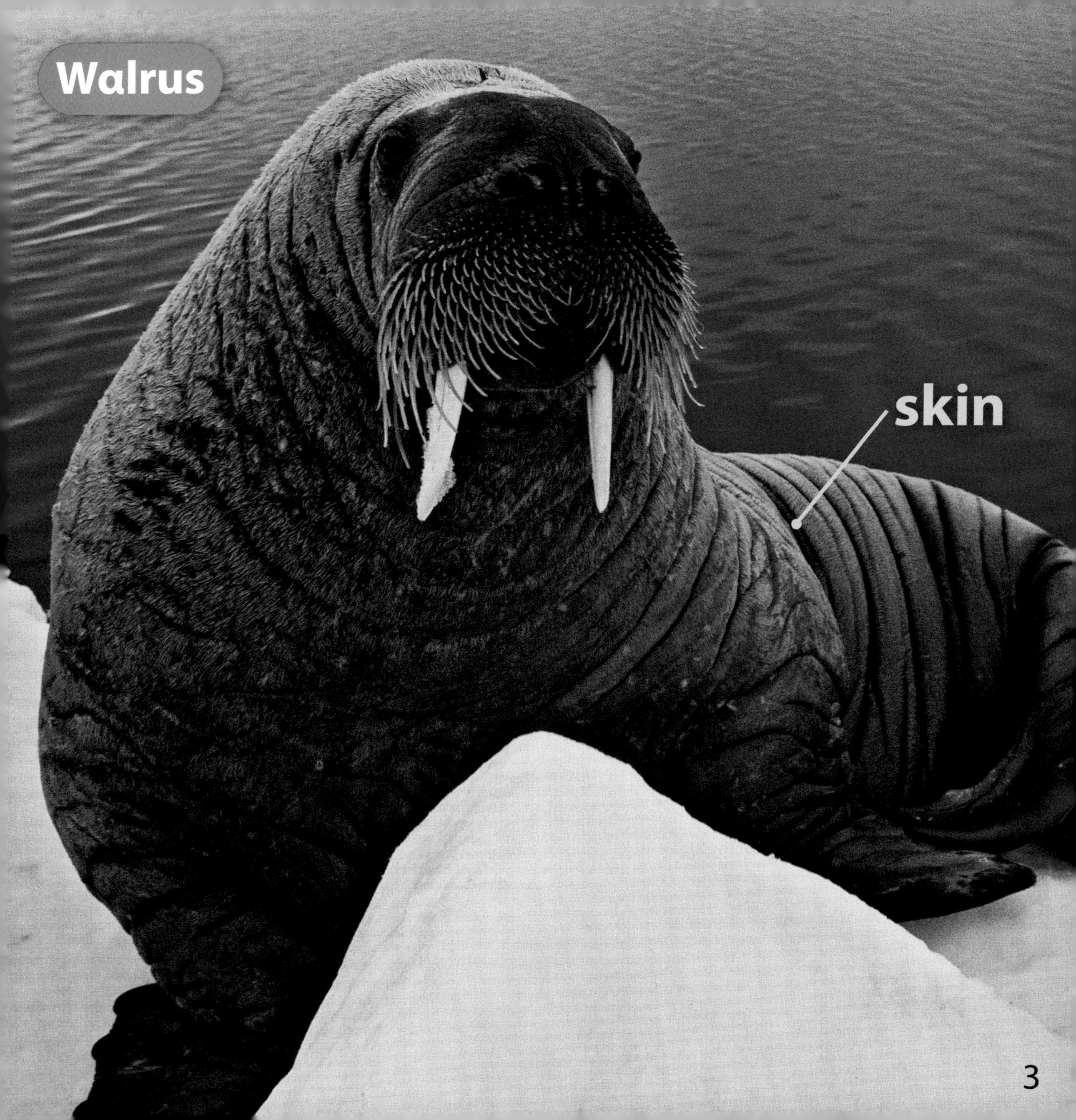
Walrus
skin

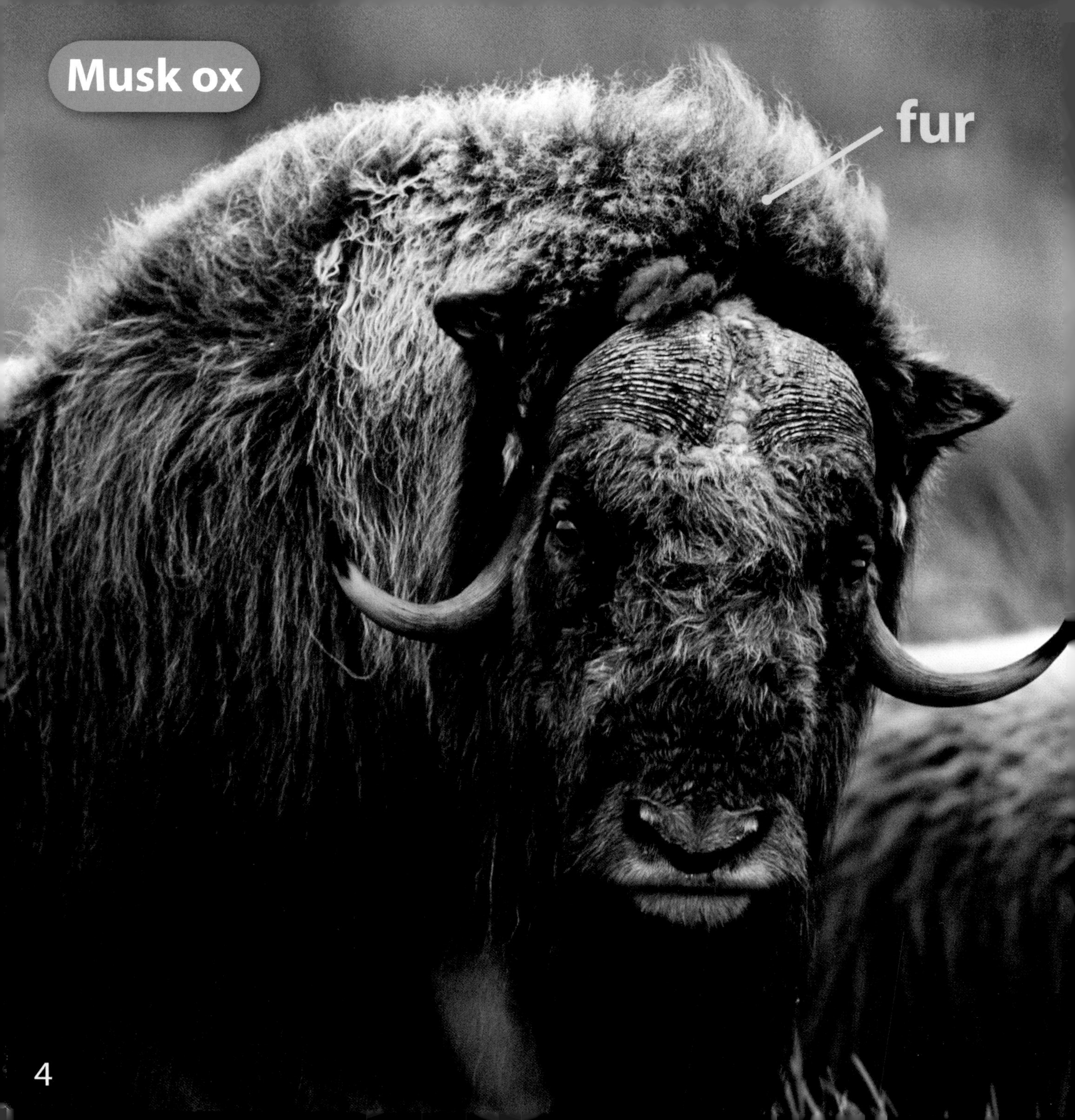
Musk ox
fur

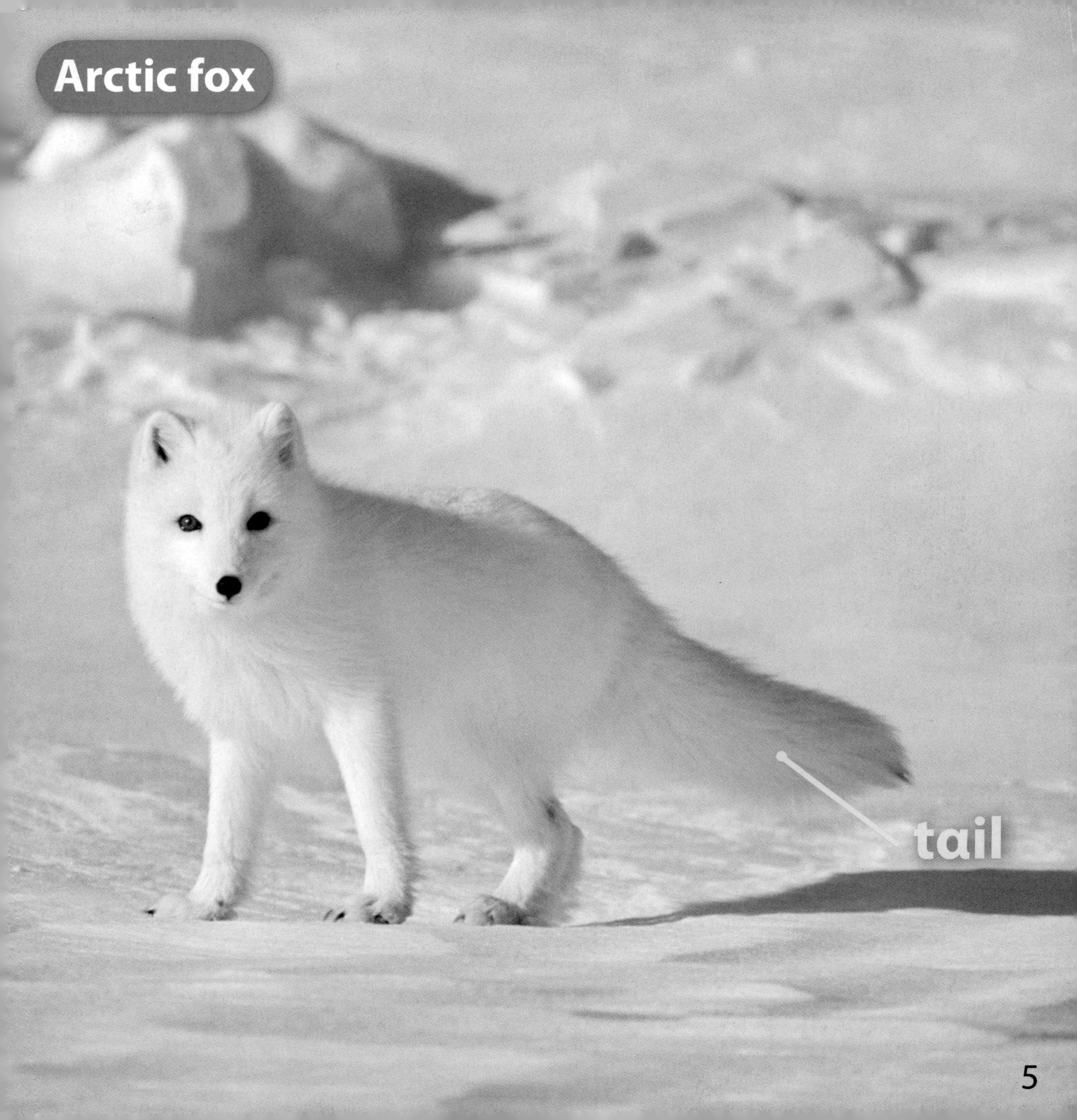
Arctic fox
tail

Fish

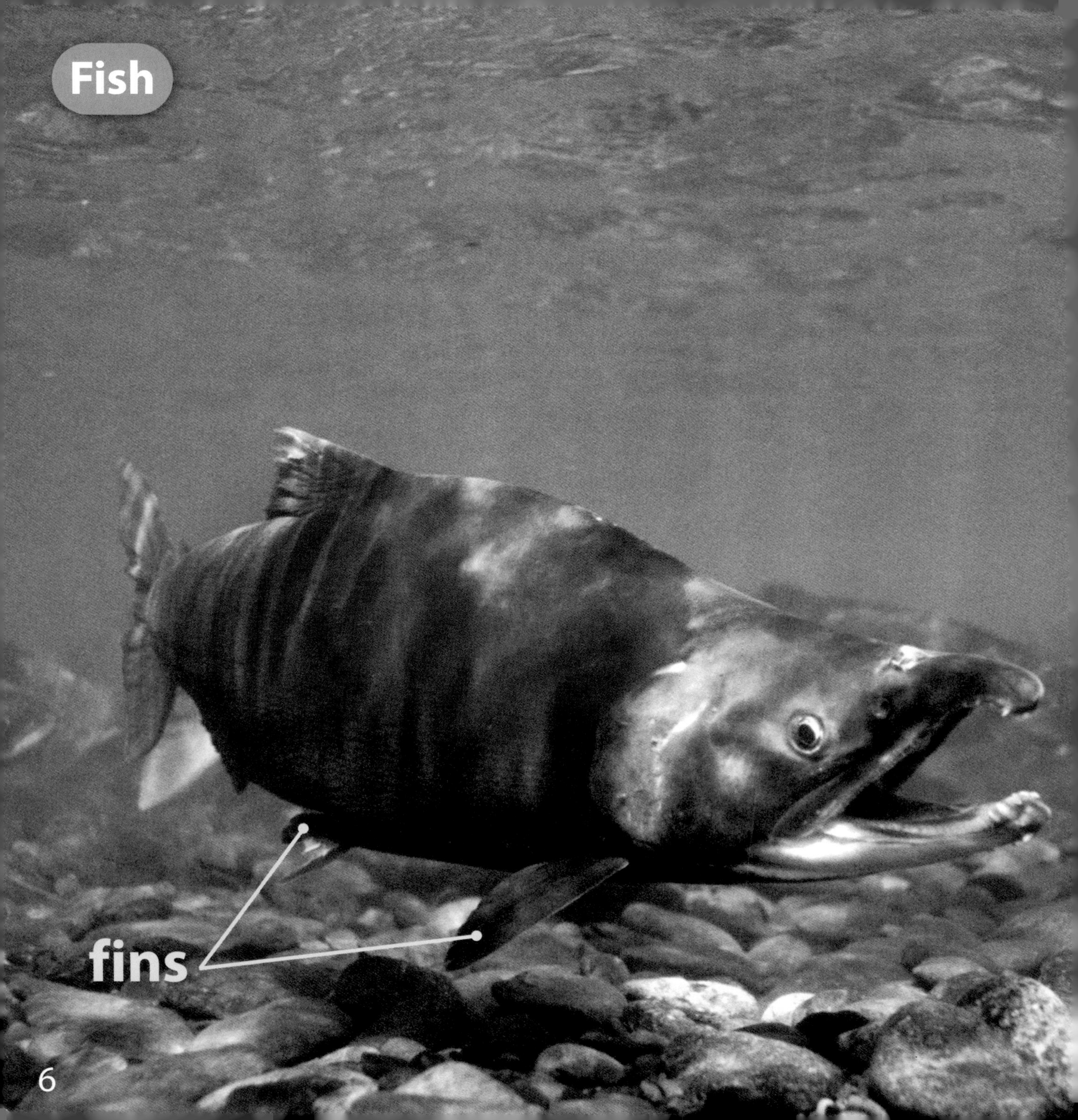

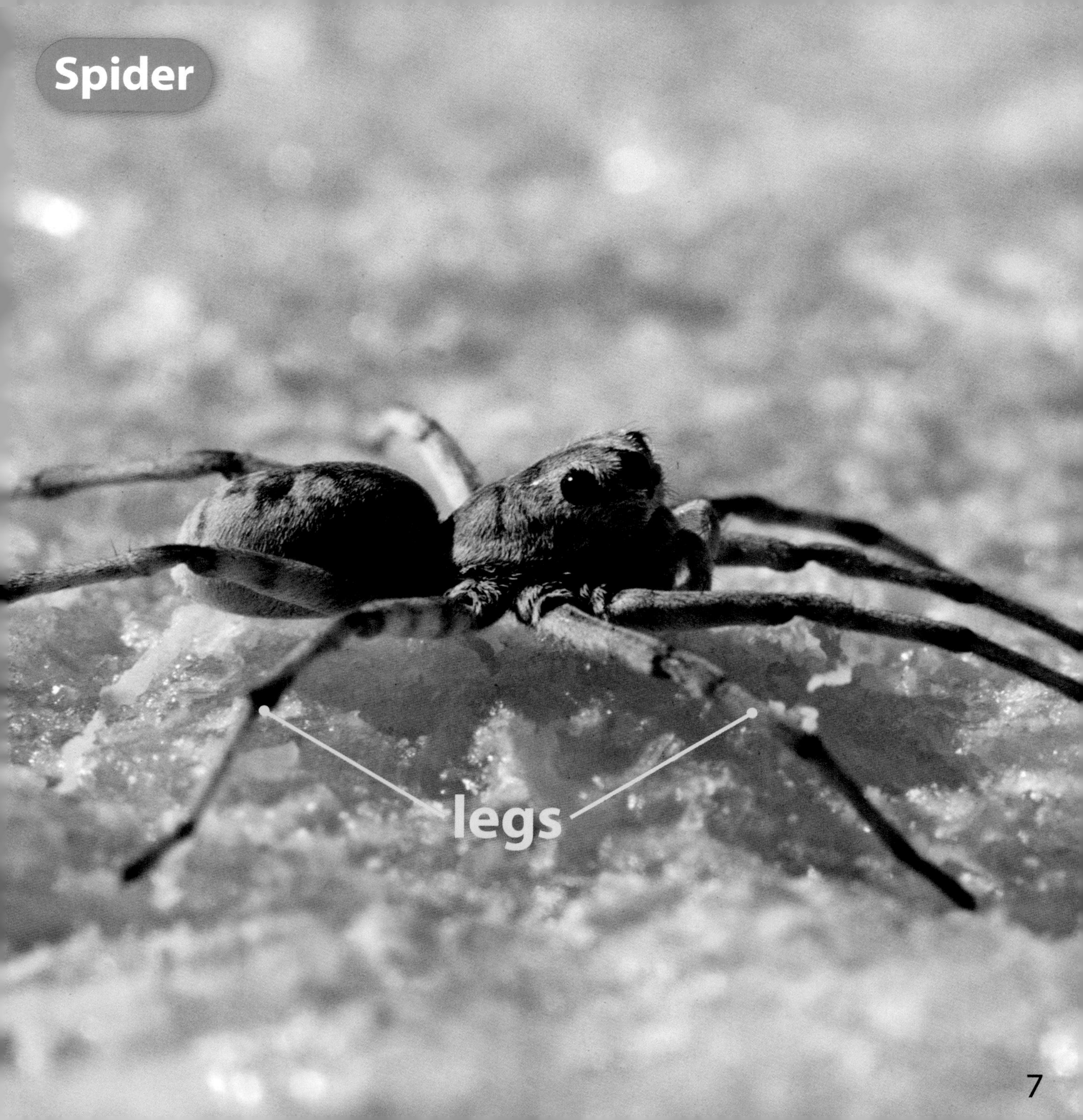
Spider
legs

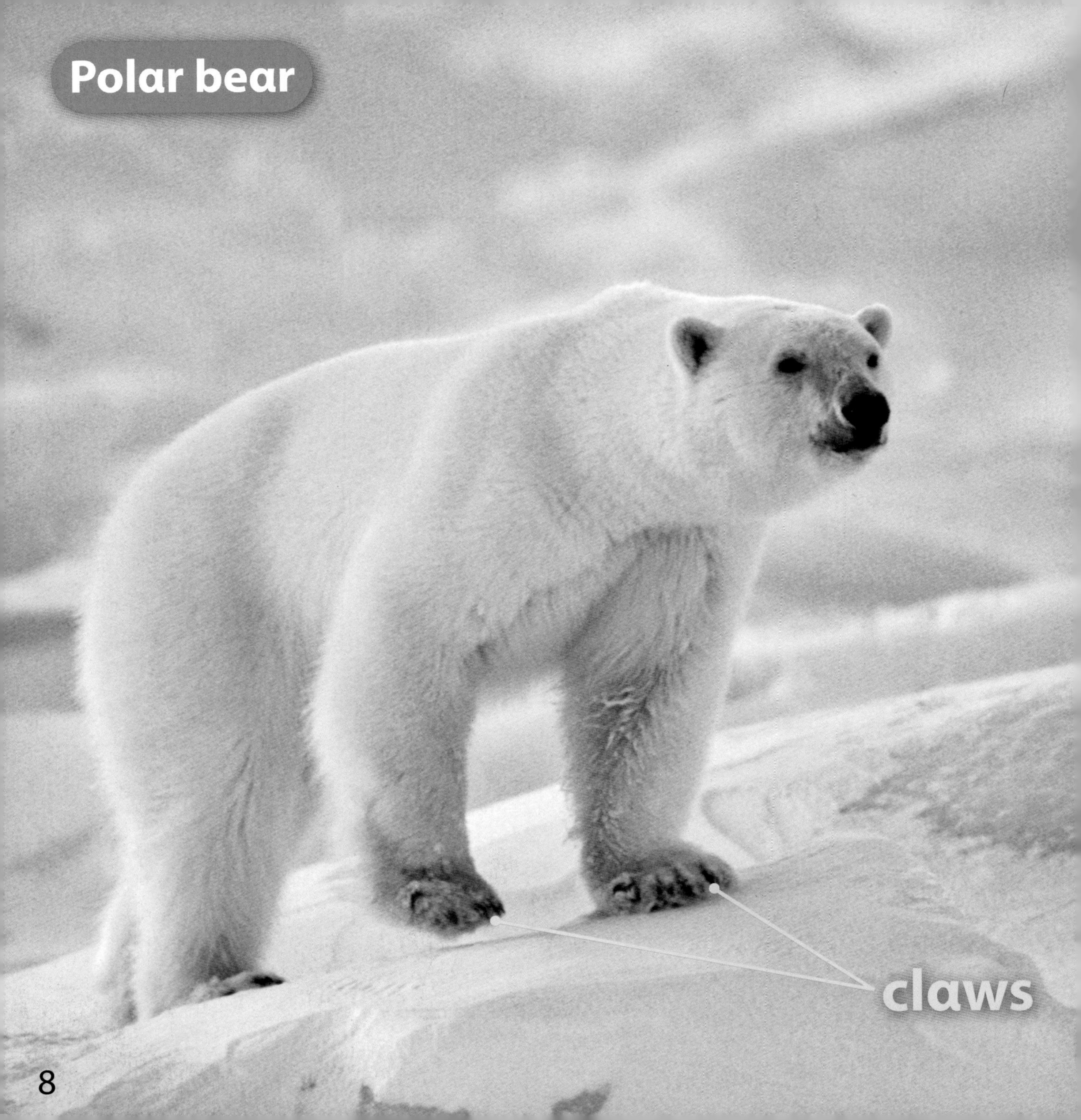
Polar bear
claws